My Little COMPASSIONATE COMPASS

PETER PAUPER PRESS, INC.
Rye Brook, New York

PETER PAUPER PRESS

In 1928, at the age of twenty-two, Peter Beilenson began printing books on a small press in the basement of his parents' home in Larchmont, New York. Peter—and later, his wife, Edna—sought to create fine books that sold at "prices even a pauper could afford."

Today, still family owned and operated, Peter Pauper Press continues to honor our founders' legacy of quality, value, and fun for big kids and small kids alike.

Written by Hannah Beilenson
Designed by Heather Zschock

3 International Drive
Rye Brook, NY 10573 USA

Published in the UK and Europe by Peter Pauper Press, Inc.
c/o White Pebble International
Units 2-3, Spring Business Park
Stanbridge Road
Havant, Hampshire PO9 2GJ, UK

ISBN 978-1-4413-4209-6
Printed in China

7 6 5 4 3 2 1

OUR ACTIONS AND US

Have you ever tried something new? Shared a toy or snack? Given a hug or high five when someone needed it? Well, those are just a few examples of putting your feelings into action! And every action you take can make a change. You can make people smile and laugh, help others feel safe, and create something new for everyone to share. There's so much you can do, and there's no wrong place to start—so let's take action today!

One action is **Compassion**, and we'll meet someone who will help us learn more about it.

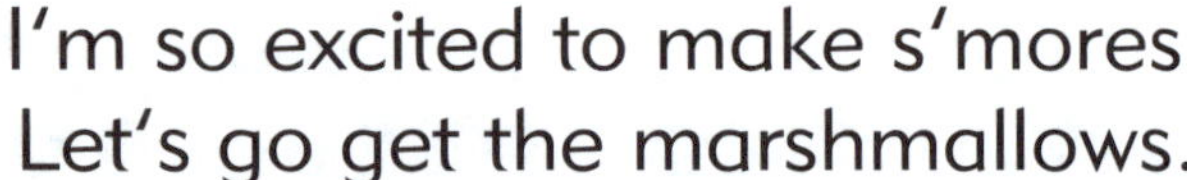

No way, I don't want to leave the fire. It's dark and scary.

Don't be a baby!
It's not that far.
Hey—that doesn't sound
very compassionate.

Who are you?
I'm a **Compassionate Compass**. I help guide you toward empathy and kindness.

Empathy—what's that?
It's when you see things from someone else's point of view, and try to understand how they feel.

Well, can you remember a time when someone you know was sad?

Yeah. My friend was sad when she lost her stuffed bear. I know how that feels.

Because I get upset
when I lose my toys, too.
So, I understand how
bad it feels.

That's empathy!
Oh, I think I'm starting to get it.

When my classmate is nervous about a talent show, I know how that feels because I've also been nervous before.

And, when my
brother is excited
about a new toy,
I'm excited too,
because I know
how fun it is to
play with some-
thing new.

That's me feeling empathy! So, it's kind of like sharing a feeling with another person?
Exactly!

And I know how scary the dark can be.
I shouldn't have been mean about it.

What do I do now?

Empathy is the first step. Then you can show compassion—it's when you put that empathy into action.

you use your Compassionate
Compass to find a way to help,
however you can.

Well, I think it probably hurt my friend's feelings when I called her a baby. And when my feelings are hurt, it helps when the other person says "Sorry." I think I should apologize.

I'm sorry for calling you a baby—it wasn't nice.
I understand why you would be afraid of the dark.

Thanks.
It's okay!

I can go get the marshmallows, and you can stay by the fire. Would that help?
Yeah!

Thanks for guiding me toward compassion.
No problem! Now, why don't I help you find the marshmallows. They should be that way!

These s'mores are pretty good!
And showing compassion feels pretty good, too.

Meet My Compassionate Compass

My Compassionate Compass's name is:

....

I show empathy when:

....

....

....

I help others by:

....

....

....